MY FIRST PIANO *Adventure*®

FOR THE YOUNG BEGINNER

by Nancy and Randall Faber

Hi! I'm Tap, the music firefly.
See you in the pages ahead!

D1416124

This book belongs to: _____

ISBN 978-1-61677-622-0

Art Direction: Terpstra Design, San Francisco, CA
Illustrations: Lisa Perrett, Charleston, SC
Portrait Illustrations: Jaye Schlesinger, Ann Arbor, MI

Tap's Message to You

TAP

Hi! It's me, TAP.
Time to get out your pencil.
In the Writing Book, we'll be playing
music games to train our EYES and EARS.

BLINKER

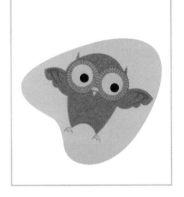

This is BLINKER, the baby owl.
She has big eyes and loves to LOOK.
Her eyes watch the page to see how music notes travel.
You'll learn that notes can **step up**, **step down**, and **repeat**.

TUCKER

This is TUCKER.
He loves to LISTEN for:
    high and low sounds
      short and long sounds
      loud and soft sounds

Let's get started. Grab your pencil and come on in!

Contents

The Glasses Store
Finger Number Review

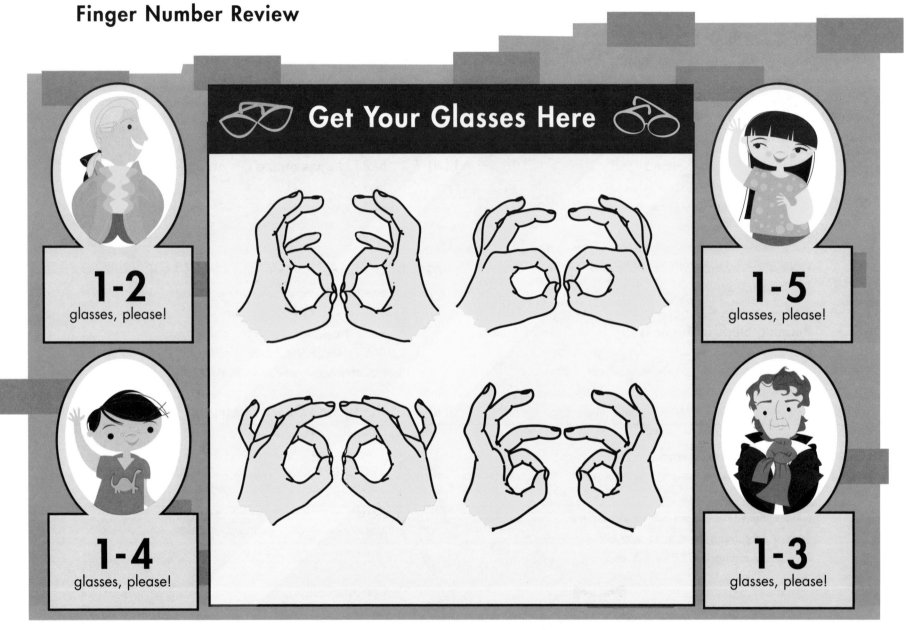

Get Your Glasses Here

1-2 glasses, please!

1-4 glasses, please!

1-5 glasses, please!

1-3 glasses, please!

1. These friends need glasses to read music.
   Connect each friend to the **matching pair of hands**.

2. Your teacher will point to one of the hands.
   See how quickly you can **copy** and **name the fingers**.

Let's Choose Glasses

Firm Fingertip Review

1. Circle the glasses that match the fingers with rings.

2. Play each row of glasses using the **C 5-finger scale** (right or left hand). Balance on *firm fingertips!*

Example: **1   1   2   2   3   3   4   4**

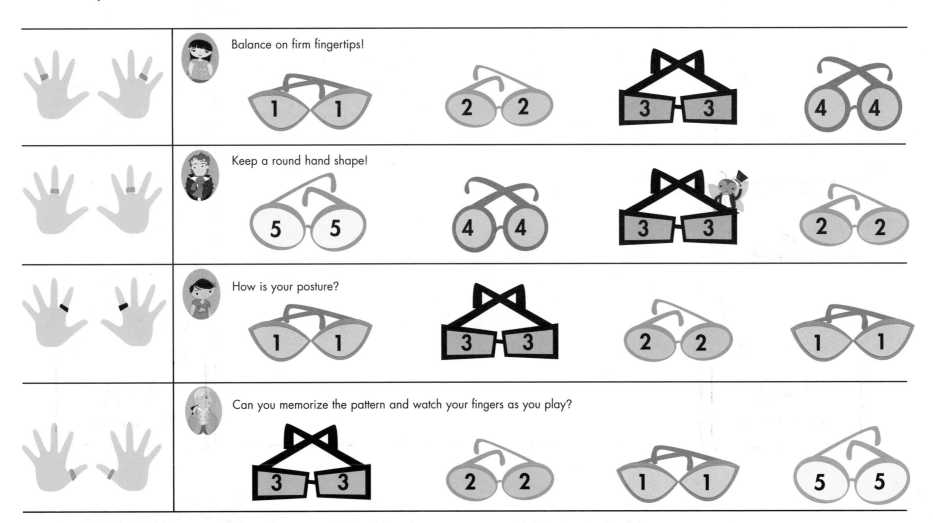

Row 1 — Balance on firm fingertips! 1 1, 2 2, 3 3, 4 4

Row 2 — Keep a round hand shape! 5 5, 4 4, 3 3, 2 2

Row 3 — How is your posture? 1 1, 3 3, 2 2, 1 1

Row 4 — Can you memorize the pattern and watch your fingers as you play? 3 3, 2 2, 1 1, 5 5

♩ Where's Tap?

**It's me, Blinker.
I love to LOOK.**

Pony Path
C 5-Finger Scale

Eye-training:

1. For each measure, circle the correct pony to show the direction of the notes.

2. Place your hands in the **C 5-finger scale** and play. Make your pony clip-clop to a steady beat!

3. Have fun playing with the duet.

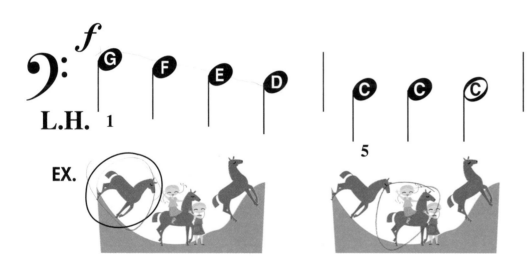

L.H. 1   5   5

EX.

Teacher Duet: (Student plays *1 octave higher.*)

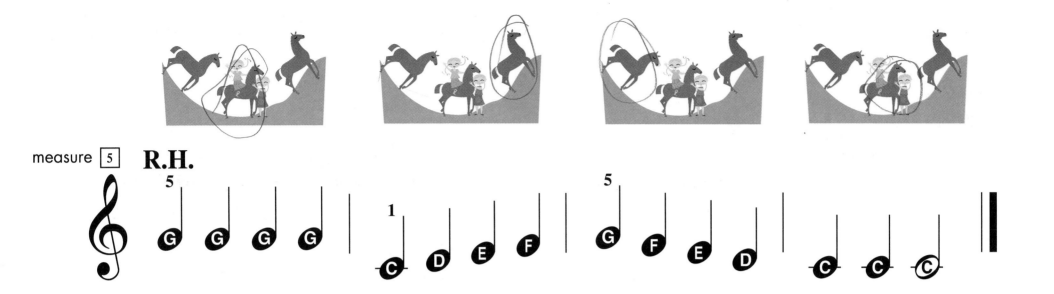

measure 5 **R.H.**

It's me, Tucker.
I love to LISTEN.

Listen! Your teacher will play a group of notes.
Say UP, DOWN, or SAME for what you hear.

For Teacher Use Only: (The examples may be played in any order. The teacher may create more examples on their own.)

How Do You Do, Mr. Beethoven?
A Touch of Music History

1. Color Beethoven's picture.

2. Draw ♩, ♩, and 𝅝 notes on the page to show notes that Beethoven might write.

Ex. ♩
1-2

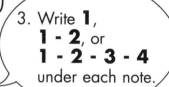

3. Write **1**, **1 - 2**, or **1 - 2 - 3 - 4** under each note.

♩ Where's Tap?

Beethoven's
Fun Facts and Game

Beethoven's Message:

"There are a thousand princes; there is only one Beethoven."

Circle each letter in Beethoven's name that is a note in music.

Ex.

L U (D) W I G

V A N

B E E T H O V E N

Fun Fact: Macaroni and cheese was one of Beethoven's favorite foods.

What is one of your favorite foods?

_____

Game: Number the pictures 1 2 3 to show Beethoven growing up.

2
<u>(write)</u>

1
<u>(write)</u>

3
<u>(write)</u>

Fun Fact: By the time Beethoven was 12, he was earning a living for his family by composing and playing the organ.

What are some of the ways you help your family? (Your teacher or parent can help you write.)

_____

_____

_____

_____

Fun Fact: Beethoven composed his greatest music after he had gone deaf. Over twenty thousand people came to his funeral.

Would you like to learn more music of Mr. Beethoven?

Line-Space Game
Orientation to the Staff

1. Circle L for LINE note or S for SPACE note.

2. Next, circle the matching number for the **line note** or **space note** on the staff.

3. For each correct answer, take one point for your team—TEAM 1.

   For any "whoopsy" answer, give a point to Tucker's TEAM—Team 2. Good luck!

Go Team!

You can win!

You know the answers!

L or S

1 2 3 4 5

L or S

For the bass clef, count TOP to BOTTOM.

1 2 3 4 5

L or S

1 2 3 4 5

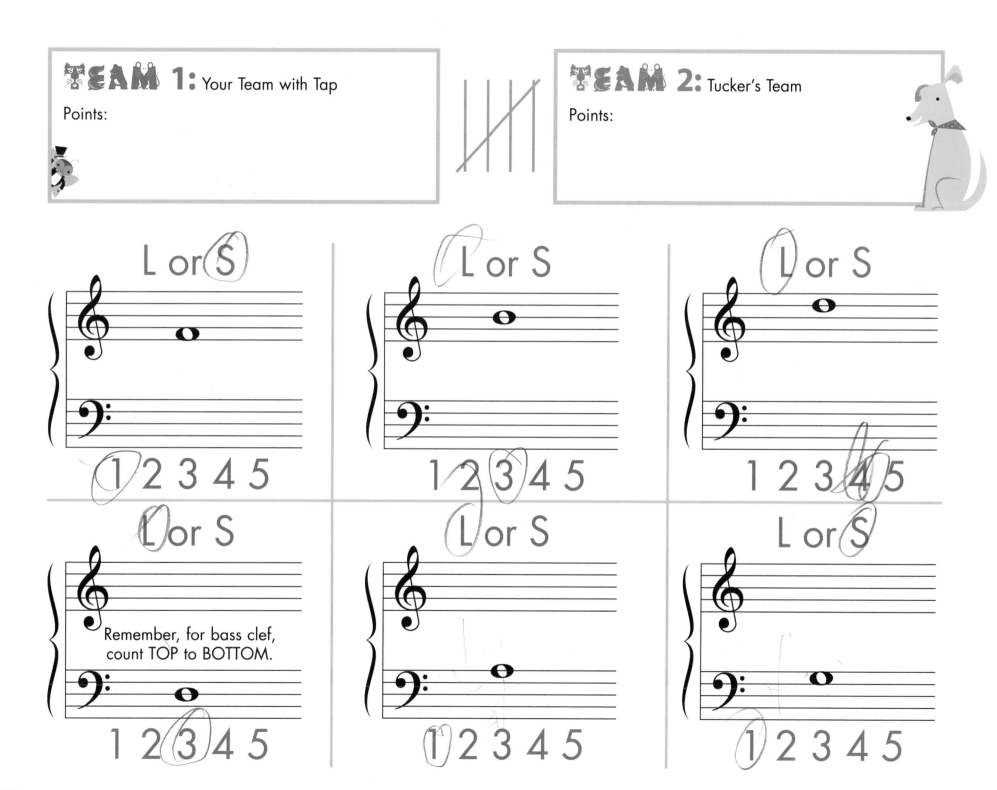

The King "Jams" with Middle C Cat

Middle C for Left Hand

 Middle C Cat has a whisker that turns it into a **line note**.

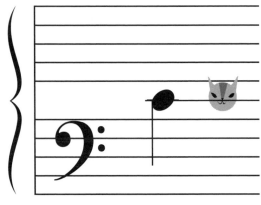

MIDDLE C

DOWN stem = L.H.

1. Draw a whisker through each note below to turn it into "Middle C Cat."

2. Draw a DOWN stem on the left for the L.H.

3. Tap and count the rhythm aloud.

4. Play with the duet for the King's party. Then make up more "jammin" rhythms on C with the duet.

Repeat using **finger 3.**

With a great beat

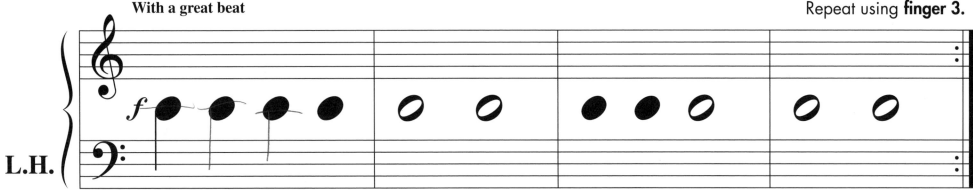

L.H.

2

Teacher Duet: (Student plays *as written.*)

Repeat for student's "jammin' rhythms."

The Queen Has Tea with Middle C Cat

Middle C for Right Hand

MIDDLE C

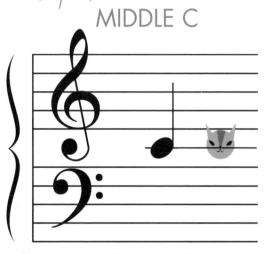

UP stem = R.H.

1. Draw a whisker through each note below to turn it into "Middle C Cat."

2. Draw an UP stem on the right for the R.H.

3. Tap and count the rhythm aloud.

4. Play with the duet to entertain the Queen.

Cheerfully

Repeat using **finger 3.**

R.H.

2

p Tea, tea,   pour the tea,   from my roy - al   tea - pot.

Teacher Duet: (Student plays *as written.*)

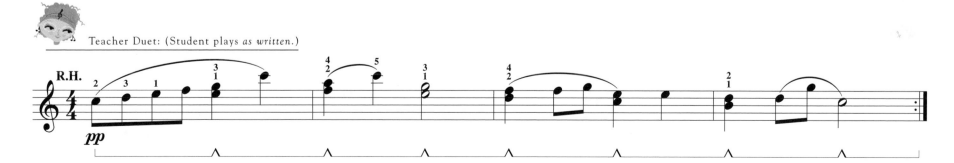

R.H.

2   3   1   3   4   5   3   4   2
      1   2   1   1   2   1

pp

Dog Bone D's
Middle D on the Treble Staff

Treble Clef D
hangs off the treble clef.
It's a space note!

That's me!

Draw a whole note
treble clef D.

1. Circle each bone with "dog bone" **D notes**.

2. Play each "bone." Use any R.H. finger.

3. Draw a line to connect the bones with the SAME RHYTHM PATTERN.
   Hint: The note names may be different—the rhythm will be the same.

Tucker's Boogie on C and D
Two-Note Improvisation

improvise—to make up

Tips from Tucker:

1. Set **R.H. fingers 2-3** on the **C-D** keys.
   First, feel the beat of the teacher duet.

2. Then create your own **C-D tune**.
   Try quick sounds and long sounds!
   Try *forte* and *piano* sounds!

3. To end, play higher C-D keys.
   End on C!

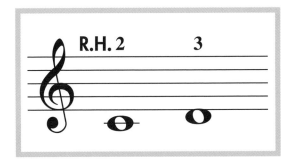

After Tucker's bath, he loves to shake and boogie!

Teacher Duet: (Student plays as *written* and on *higher* C-D keys.)

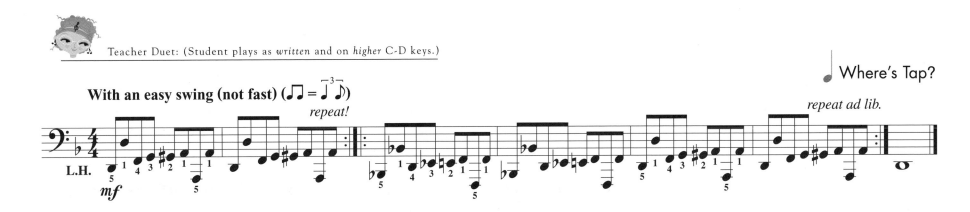

With an easy swing (not fast)

repeat!   *repeat ad lib.*

Where's Tap?

L.H.   *mf*

Fish Can't Step, or Can They?

Stepping Up and Down

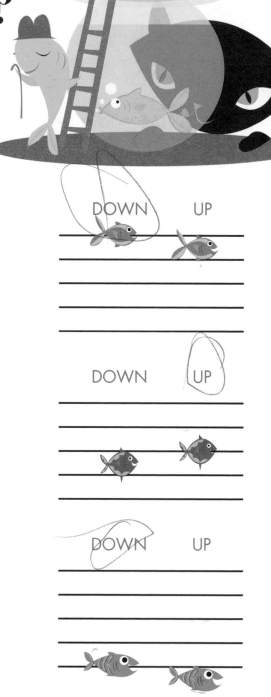

1. Circle DOWN or UP to show which way the fish are stepping.

2. Your teacher will play a step on the piano.*
   Listen, then sing with your teacher "step up" or "step down."

DOWN ~~UP~~

DOWN ~~UP~~

~~DOWN~~ UP

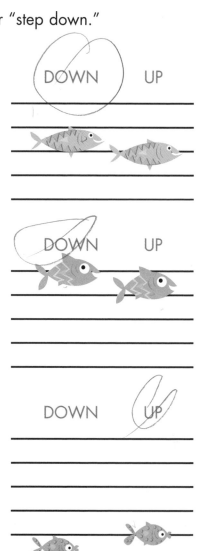

~~DOWN~~ UP

~~DOWN~~ UP

DOWN ~~UP~~

DOWN ~~UP~~

DOWN ~~UP~~

~~DOWN~~ UP

*Teacher Note: For the child's vocal range, play steps between Middle C and Treble C. Ex. D-E, G-F, A-B, A-G.
It may be helpful for you and the student to shape the sound (pitch) in the air with your hands.

Mrs. Razzle-Dazzle's Stepping Path

Discovering Steps

Mrs. Razzle-Dazzle has a goldfish pond.

1. Circle the musical **steps** on the path.
   Think LINE to a SPACE or SPACE to a LINE.

2. Can you draw a "happy face" under the 3
   stepping stones that use **only Middle C's**?

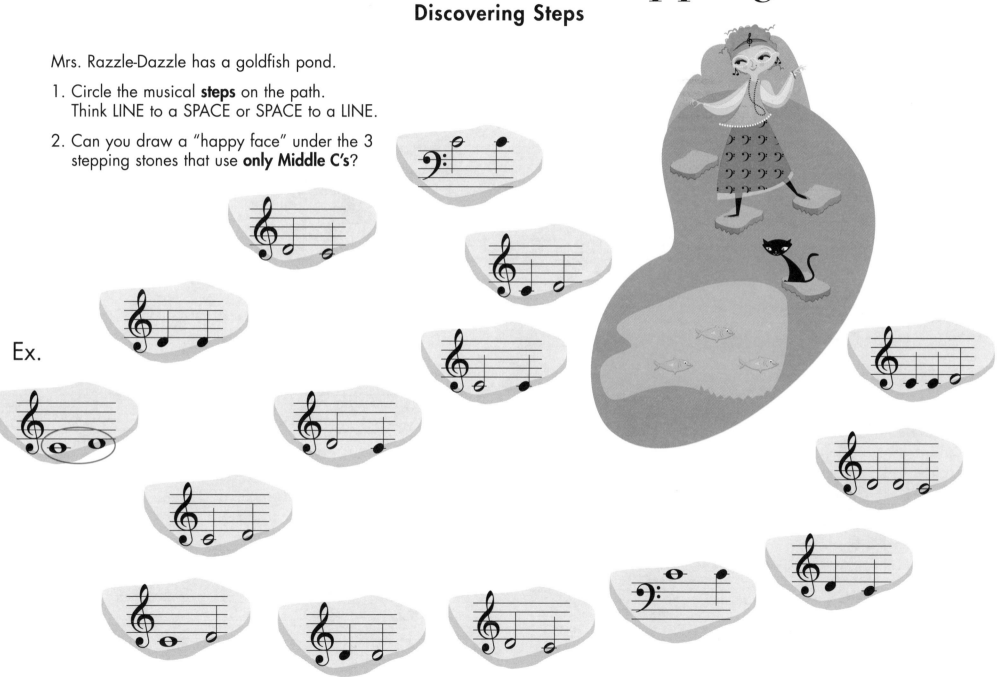

Leaf Pile Fun
Middle E on the Treble Staff

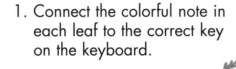

Treble Clef E

sits on **line 1** of the treble clef.

That's me!

Draw a whole note **treble clef E**.

1. Connect the colorful note in each leaf to the correct key on the keyboard.

2. Play the notes in each leaf on the piano.

♩ Where's Tap?

LISTEN

Ear-training:

1. Circle the **rhythm** your teacher taps. (The teacher chooses **a** or **b**.)
Then reverse. You tap and let your teacher guess the rhythm.

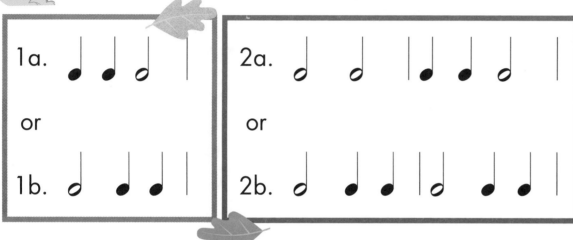

2. Circle the melody your teacher plays. (The teacher chooses **a** or **b**.)
Hint: Watch for repeated notes!

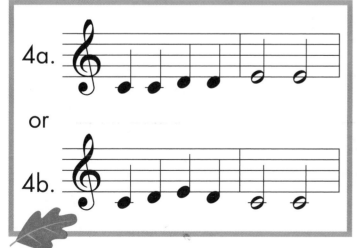

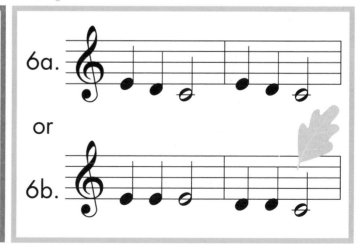

LOOK

CLAP for Sightreading

The word *sightreading* means to play through a piece for the first time.

Follow these 4 steps.

Eye-training:

1. **COUNT** and clap the rhythm.

2. **LOOK** at the first note. Is it on a line or space? Find it on the piano.

3. **ATTENTION** on what's next! Up, down, or same?

4. **PLAY.** To begin, set a steady beat by saying "1-2-3 GO."

C — Count

L — Look

A — Attention

P — Play

Hint: Keep your eyes on the music. Notice the **forte** sign!

1 *on __?*

Hint: Notice the *piano* sign!

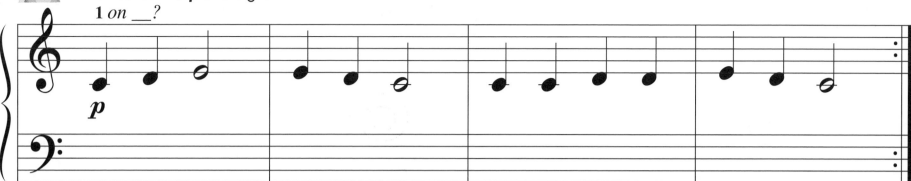

2

 Hint: Notice the **echo** in *measure 2.*

3

 Hint: *Feel* the **two** beats in the half notes. *Feel* the **four** beats in the whole notes.

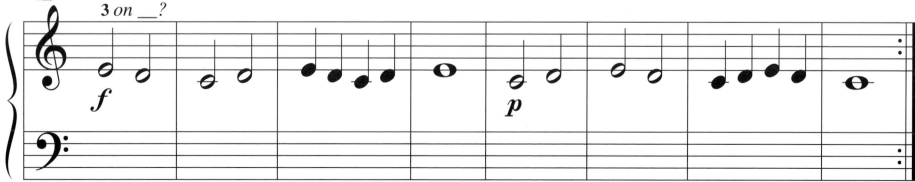

4

♩ Where's Tap?

How Do You Do, Wolfgang?

A Touch of Music History

1. Color Mozart's picture.

2. Write a different **rhythm pattern** in each measure. See the sample patterns below.

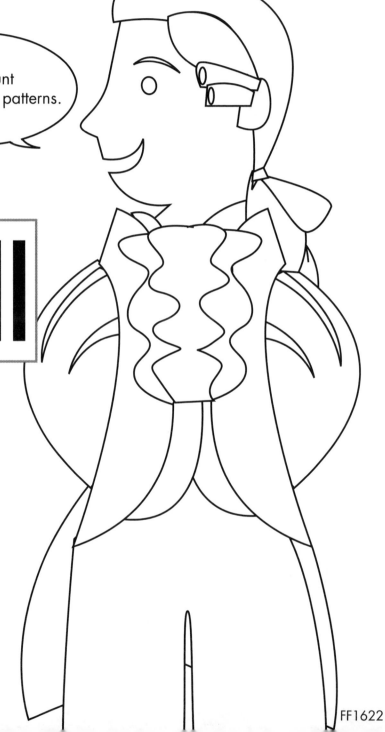

3. Tap and count your rhythm patterns.

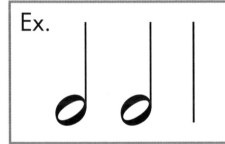

(you write)

Sample Rhythm Patterns

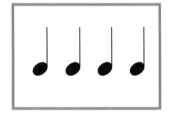 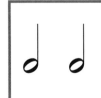  

Mozart's
Fun Facts and Game

Fun Fact: Mozart's full name was Joannes Chrysostomus Wolfgangus Theaphilus Mozart. He preferred Wolfgang Amadeus Mozart.

What is your full name?

_____

_____

_____

Mozart's Message to You:

We can do no great things; only small things with great love.
—Wolfgang Amadeus Mozart

Can you think of a small thing someone has kindly done for you or you for them? (Your teacher or parent can help you write.)

_____

_____

_____

Game: Find and circle the name MOZART 5 times. Look down, across, and backward!

M	T	M	E	U	M	M
O	U	N	G	R	O	O
Z	T	R	S	M	Z	Z
A	R	T	U	O	A	A
R	A	X	G	Z	R	R
T	Z	H	R	A	T	T
M	O	Z	A	R	T	—
P	M	V	T	T	X	—

Fun Fact: When Mozart was learning math, he would fill the walls and floors of his room with numbers written with chalk.

Draw the music note that matches this number of beats.

Fun Fact: Mozart loved to play cards.

Draw a big **whole note** around the cards if you like to play, too!

Fun Fact: When Mozart was 3, he spent much time playing skips at the piano. For example, **C-E**.

Your teacher will help you play some skips on the piano. Do you find the sound pleasing like Mozart?

Tooth Fairy Visit
A on the Bass Staff

Bass Clef A
is the TOP line
in the bass clef.

That's me!

Draw a whole note
bass clef A.

Connect each tooth to the correct pillow.

♩ Where's Tap?

$\textit{mf}$ mezzo forte means moderately loud

LISTEN

Ear-training:

Your teacher will play a musical example.
Listen carefully! Was the example f, mf, or p?

1. f or mf or p 2. f or mf or p 3. f or mf or p

4. f or mf or p 5. f or mf or p 6. f or mf or p

 For Teacher Use Only: (The examples may be played p, mf, or f, and "played" in any order.)

Lightly Row

March Slav

Jingle Bells

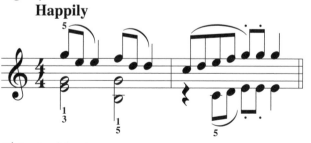

Skip to My Lou

Twinkle, Twinkle Little Star

Beethoven's 5th Symphony

Treasure Hunt
B on the Bass Staff

12/3

Bass Clef B
is the space note that sits on top of the bass staff.

That's me!

Draw a whole note **bass clef B**.

1. Use yellow to color the coins with **bass clef B's**.
2. How many gold coins do you have? _____

3. How many **bass clef B's** are in each short melody?

 2

 1

 2

2 2

LOOK

Eye-training:
Sightread the examples above.

FF1622

A-B-C-D-E Rock!
Five-Note Improvisation

improvise—to make up

Tips from Mrs. Razzle-Dazzle:

1. First, set your fingers over these keys. Listen and feel the beat as your teacher plays the duet.

2. Now *improvise* your own **A-B-C-D-E tune** with the duet. Use the keys in any order!

3. To end, your teacher will chant, "Now, play an A key, it's the end!"

(Teacher Note: See final two measures.)

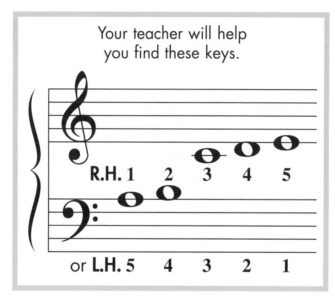

Your teacher will help you find these keys.

R.H. 1   2   3   4   5

or **L.H.** 5   4   3   2   1

Let's improvise! Feel the beat!

Teacher Duet: (Student plays as written.)

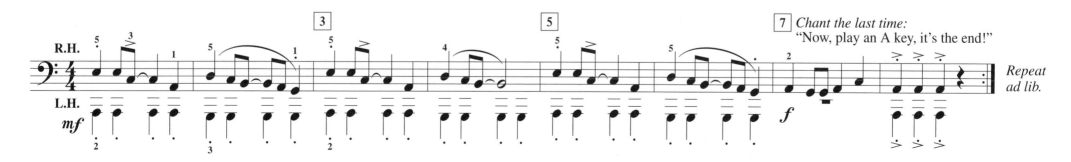

7 *Chant the last time:* "Now, play an A key, it's the end!"

Repeat ad lib.

Sailor Note Friend
Creating with Note Values

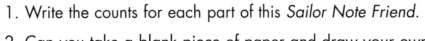

Dotted Half Note

3 counts

count **1 - 2 - 3**

- Draw **dotted half notes** all over this box!

- Write 1 2 3 under each note.

1. Write the counts for each part of this *Sailor Note Friend*.

2. Can you take a blank piece of paper and draw your own "note friend"?

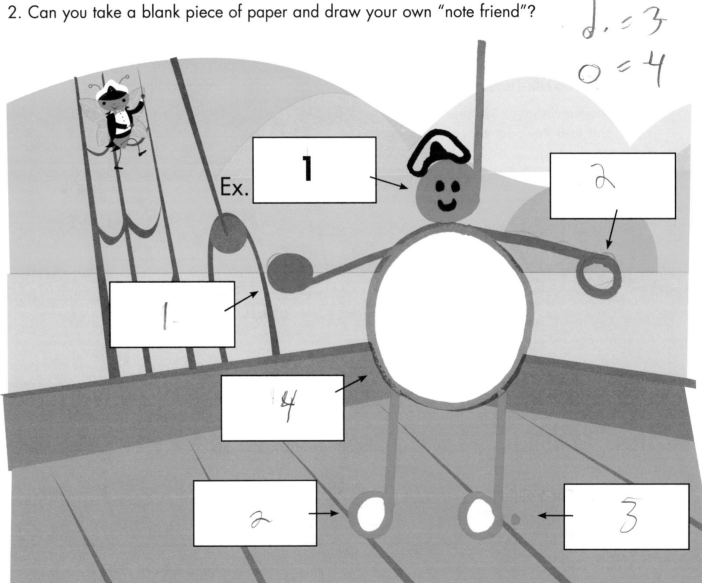

Long May They Wave!
Finding Rhythm Patterns

LOOK

Eye-training:

Each flag has another flag with the **same rhythm pattern**.

1. Draw a line connecting the matching flags.

2. Tap the **rhythm pattern** in each flag.

Ex.

LISTEN

Ear-training:

3. Your teacher will count "1-2-3-4" and then tap one of these rhythm patterns.

Point to a flag with the rhythm you hear.

Where's Tap now?

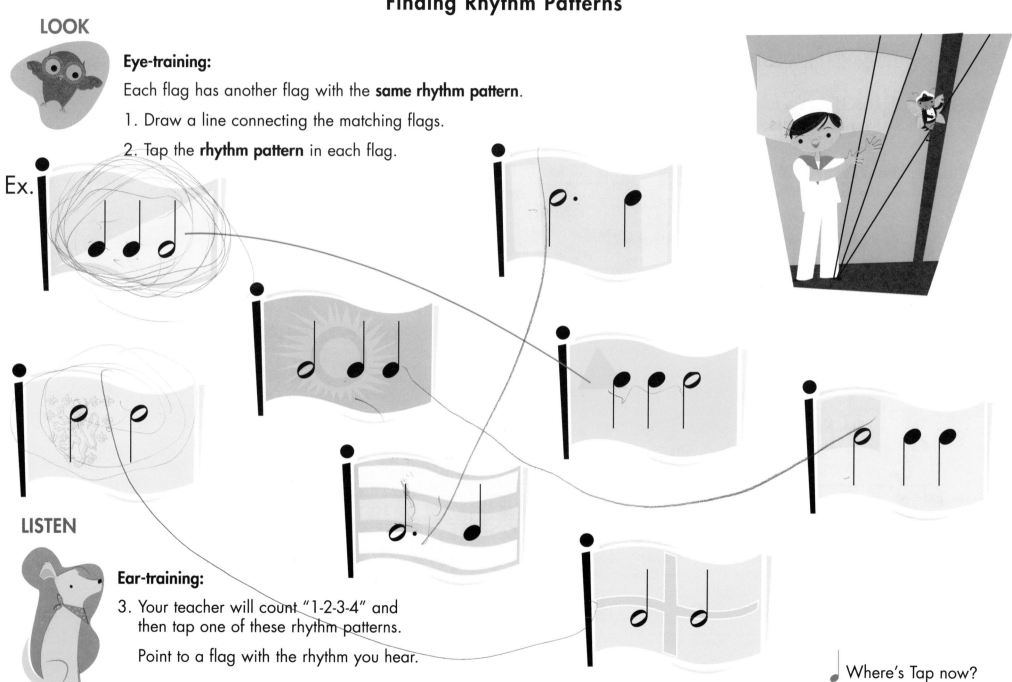

LOOK

Remember these 4 steps for sightreading.

Eye-training:

1. **COUNT** and clap the rhythm.

2. **LOOK** at the first note. Is it on a line or space? Find it on the piano.

3. **ATTENTION** on what's next! Up, down, or same?

4. **PLAY.** To begin, set a steady beat by saying "1-2-3 GO."

CLAP for Sightreading

C = ?

L = ?

A = ?

P = ?

Hint: Keep your eyes on the music!
Be sure to count **1-2-3** for each dotted half note.

1 on __?

1

mf

2 on __?

Hint: Be sure to count **1-2-3-4** for each whole note.

3 *on* ___?

2

f-p *on repeat*

(1 - 2 - 3 - 4)   *(1 - 2 - 3 - 4)*

2 *on* ___?

Hint: Be sure to count **1-2** for each half note.

1 *on* ___?

3

mf

3 *on* ___?   **1**

Hint: Be sure to keep a steady quarter-note beat!

3 *on* ___?

4

mf

2 *on* ___?

♩ Where's Tap?

Escape of the Quarter Notes!
Rhythm Activity

(Directions on p. 33)

Time Signature

4 counts in a measure

the quarter note gets 1 beat

- Draw this **time signature** below.

- Can you turn the lower 4 into a quarter note?

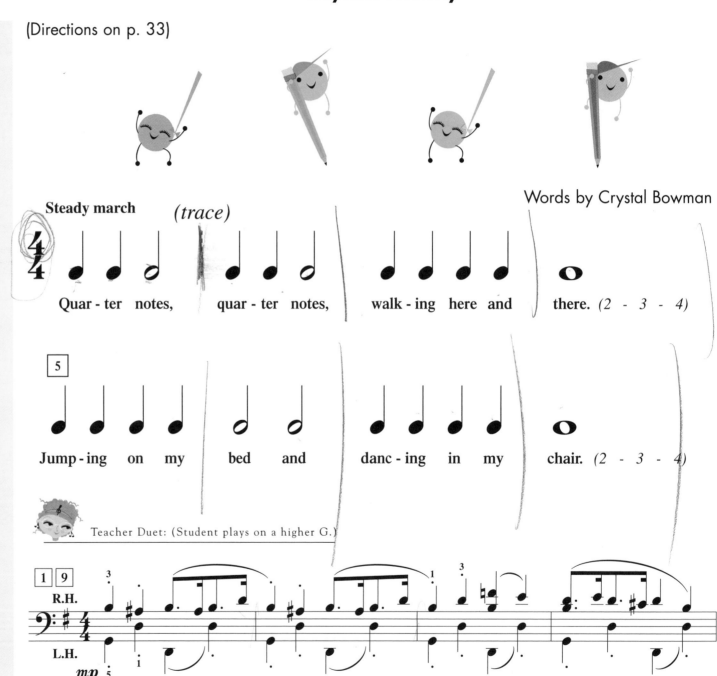

Words by Crystal Bowman

Steady march *(trace)*

Quar - ter notes, quar - ter notes, walk - ing here and there. *(2 - 3 - 4)*

5

Jump - ing on my bed and danc - ing in my chair. *(2 - 3 - 4)*

Teacher Duet: (Student plays on a higher G.)

1 9

R.H.

L.H. *mp*

1. Draw a bar line every **4 beats**.

2. Next, tap the rhythm with your teacher
as he/she chants the words.

3. Now, play the rhythm on a **G key** while your teacher
plays the duet. Use finger 3 braced with the thumb.

9

Quar - ter notes, quar - ter notes, ev - 'ry - where I look. *(2 - 3 - 4)*

13

How did they es - cape from my pi - an - o book? *(2 - 3 - 4)*

Horse and Saddles

G on the Bass Staff

Bass Clef G
is the top SPACE
in the bass clef.

That's me!

Draw a whole note
bass clef G.

1. Circle all the saddles with **bass clef G's**.

   Hint: Think "A is the top line,
   step down to ____?"

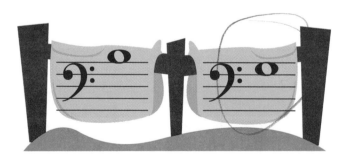

2. Play and say the rhythm of **your name** on bass clef G.
   Use any L.H. finger. Your teacher will go first.

♩ Where's Tap?

Tips from Tap:

1. Do these 3 hand signals with your teacher and say the **letter names** aloud.

2. Now, sing this song with your teacher and do the "secret hand signals" for each note. Do this at many lessons!

3. Your teacher will do a hand signal. Name the note. Then reverse!

Secret Hand Signals
Bass Clef G-A-B

A is the *top* line in the bass clef.

Signal A
Flat hand

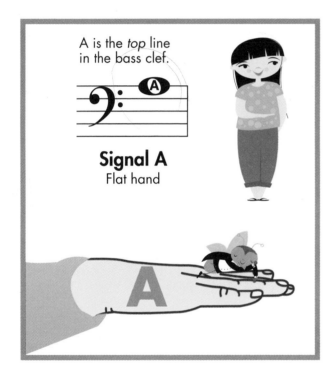

G is the space *below* top line A.

Signal G
Fist BELOW flat hand

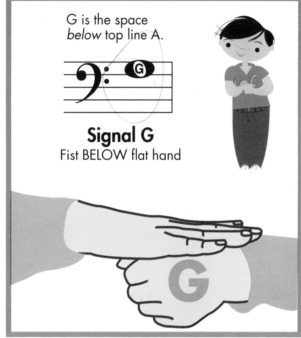

B is the space *above* top line A.

Signal B
Fist ABOVE flat hand

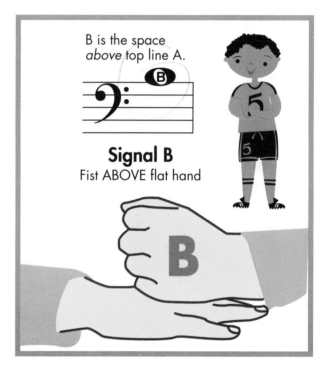

 Teacher melody to sing. (The melody may be sung as is or sung an octave higher.)

Quickly

A is the top line, step down to G. A is the top line, step up to B. A is the top line, step down to G. A, B, A, G, A!

Queen of the Sea

Rhythm Activity

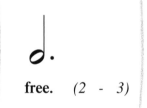

1. Draw a bar line every **3 beats**.

2. Next, tap the rhythm with your teacher as he/she chants the words.

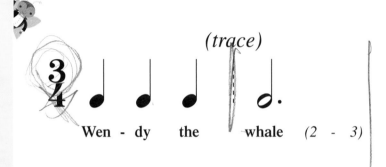

(trace)

Wen - dy   the   whale   *(2 - 3)*   Wen - dy   the   whale   *(2 - 3)*

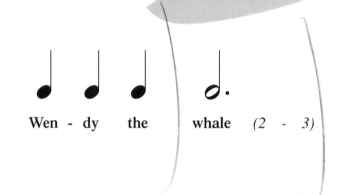

5

Deep   in   the   sea   you   swim   wild   and   free.   *(2 - 3)*

LISTEN

Ear-training:

Do *Queen of the Sea* as a "rhythm round." You start by tapping and saying, "1, 1, 1," etc. At **measure 5**, your teacher will begin. (Take the repeat.)

♩ Where's Tap?

Tips from Tap:

1. Write the correct **time signature** before each rhythm.

2. Then choose any key and play each rhythm on the piano.

Rhythm Fun
Finding the Time Signature

LISTEN

Ear-training:

Your teacher will tap or play one of the rhythms above. Point to the one you hear.

True or False?

Directional Reading

1. Circle TRUE or FALSE for each example.

2. If the answer is FALSE, tell your teacher the correct answer.

Treble Clef F
is the first SPACE
in the treble clef.

That's me!

Draw a whole note
treble clef F.

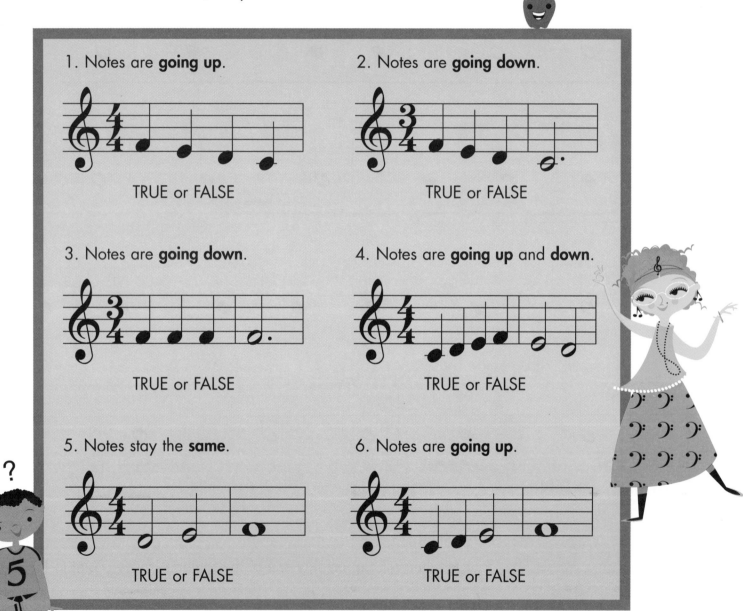

1. Notes are **going up**.

TRUE or FALSE

2. Notes are **going down**.

TRUE or FALSE

3. Notes are **going down**.

TRUE or FALSE

4. Notes are **going up** and **down**.

TRUE or FALSE

5. Notes stay the **same**.

TRUE or FALSE

6. Notes are **going up**.

TRUE or FALSE

LISTEN

Ear-training:

Your teacher will play two short melodies.
Listen! If they are the **same**, circle the two apples.
If they are **different**, circle the apple and orange.

Apples or Oranges

Hearing Same or Different

1.

2.

3.

4.

5.

6.

For Teacher Use Only: (The examples may be played in any order. The teacher may create more "same" or "different" examples for the student.)

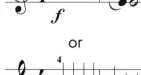

or

or

or

or

CLAP for Sightreading

LOOK

Eye-training:

Spell the word C L A P in the four boxes below.

□ **COUNT** and clap the rhythm.

□ **LOOK** at the *first* note. Is it on a line or space?
Find it on the piano.

□ **ATTENTION** on what's next!
Up, down, or same?

□ **PLAY**. To begin, set a steady beat
by saying "1-2-3 GO."

Tell your teacher what this means: $\frac{4}{4}$ Hint: Think $\frac{4}{4}$

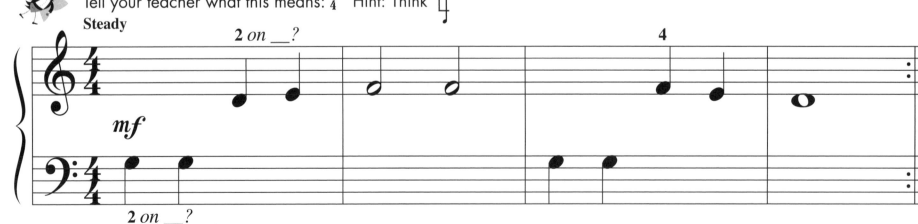

Steady

1

2 on __?

mf

2 on __?

4

Tell your teacher what this means: 3/4   Hint: Think 3/4

2

1 *on* ___?

p

1 *on* ___?

Write 3/4 or 4/4 for each staff.

3

1 *on* ___?

4

f

1 *on* ___?

Write 3/4 or 4/4 for each staff.

4

1 *on* ___?

mf

3 *on* ___?

Queen's Entrance

Improvising with Treble Clef G

Treble Clef G
is **line 2** of the treble clef.

That's me!

Draw a whole note **treble clef G**.

Pretend trumpets announce "Queen Treble Clef."

1. Use a **R.H. 3-1 donut** and find the **Treble G** key.

2. Listen to the duet. Now improvise your own Treble G rhythms. Play *forte* into the keys.

3. Did you know the 𝄞 comes from the **letter G**? Your teacher will help you draw a G over each treble clef above.

Teacher Duet: (Student improvises on **Treble G.**)

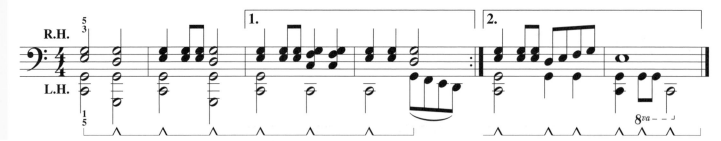

CLAP for Sightreading

LOOK

Eye-training:

1. Lightly color the measure in each row that matches the **measure on the left.**

2. Sightread the measures going across in each row to create a melody!

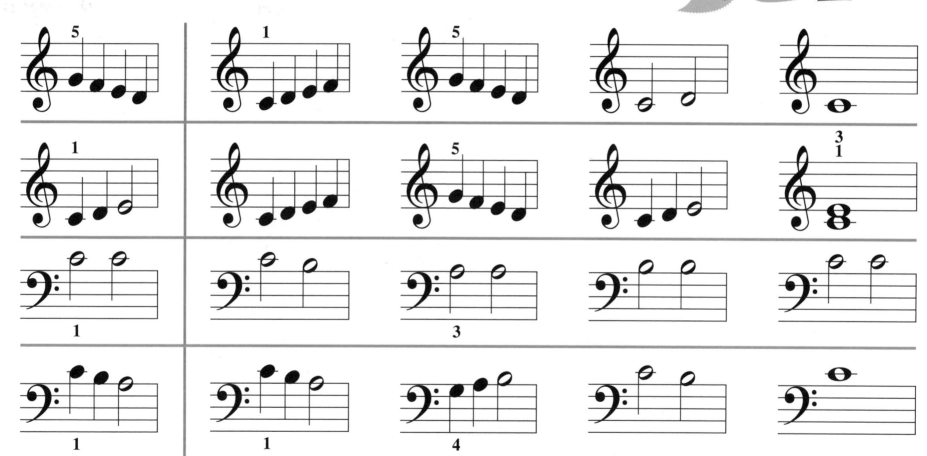

LISTEN

Ear-training:

Your teacher will play one of the lines of music.
Listen and see how fast you can point to the one played.

Beethoven's Composing Room

Review of Symbols and Terms

Welcome to my composing room.
Please take a look around!

1. Tell your teacher about each musical symbol.
   Then draw a "smiley face" by each.

1. What is this symbol?

2. Name the note.

3. A staff has 5 _____ .

4. A staff has 4 _____ .

5. Name the note.
The treble clef is also
known as the _____ clef.

6. What does this mean?

7. These are the _____ .

8. What is this called?
What does it mean?

Answers
1. treble clef
2. middle C
3. lines
4. spaces
5. treble G, G clef
6. time signature
   (3 beats in a measure, ♩ = 1 beat)
7. pedals
8. double bar line, end of the piece

9. Name the note.
Do the hand signal. (p. 35)

10. Name the note.
Do the hand signal.

11. Name the note.
Do the hand signal.

12. What does this mean?

13. Name the note.
How many beats?

14. Name the note.
How many beats?

15. Name the note.
How many beats?

16. Name the note.
How many beats?

17. Name the symbol.

18. What does this mean?

19. What does this mean?

20. What does this mean?

Answers (continued)
9. bass clef A
10. bass clef G
11. bass clef B
12. time signature
(4 beats in a measure, ♩ = 1 beat)
13. quarter note (1 beat)
14. half note (2 beats)
15. dotted half note (3 beats)
16. whole note (4 beats)
17. bass clef
18. *piano* (soft)
19. *forte* (loud)
20. *mezzo forte* (moderately loud)

♩ Where's Tap?

King's Entrance
Improvising with Bass Clef F

Bass Clef F
is the 2nd line
down on the bass clef.

That's me!

Draw a whole note
bass clef F.

Pretend trumpets announce "King Bass Clef."

1. Form a **L.H. 3-1 donut** and find the **Bass F** key.

2. Listen to the duet. Now improvise your own
   Bass F rhythms. Play *forte* into the key.

  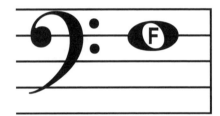

Example

3. Did you know the bass clef comes from a very old style of the **letter F**?
   Your teacher will help you draw an old style F over each bass clef above.

Teacher Duet: (Students improvise on **Bass F**.)

♩ Where's Tap?

Marching proudly

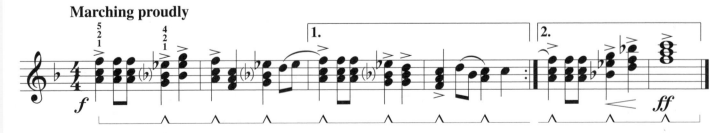

Turn to your Lesson Book, p. 62.

Point Where I Stop
Tracking the Notes

Eye-training:

1. Your teacher will play *I Would Like to Go to Mars* and STOP on any note.
   You watch the music carefully and point to the LAST note played.

2. Circle a Martian each time you point correctly!

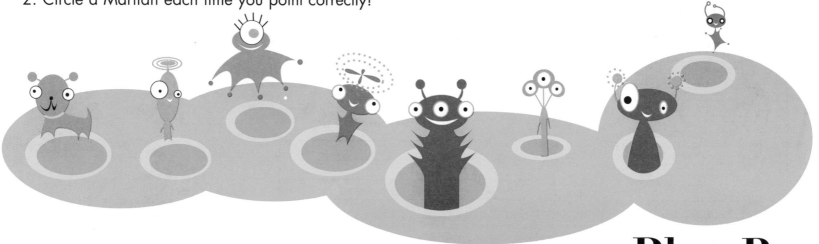

LISTEN

Ear-training:

1. Place your R.H. in the **C 5-finger scale**.
   Close your eyes and listen!

2. Your teacher will play a short set of notes on a lower C scale.
   Play back what you hear.

Play Back
Hearing Patterns

For Teacher Use Only: (The examples may be repeated several times.)
The teacher may create more examples on his/her own.

Bass C Groove
C on the Bass Staff

Bass C

is space 3
in the bass clef.
The stem goes UP.

That's me!

Draw a half note
bass C.

Review: *Improvise* means to create music "on the spot."

Improvise duets using only **Bass C** and **Middle C** notes.
The first duet is fast. The second duet is slow.

Use
3–1
donuts!

Middle **C**

Bass **C**

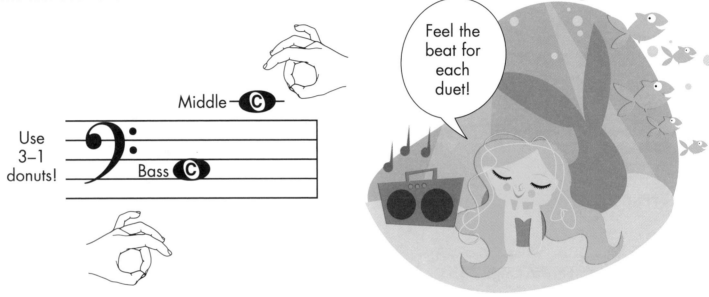

Feel the
beat for
each
duet!

Teacher Duets: (The student may enjoy improvising the waltz again using any white keys. Coach to end on C.)

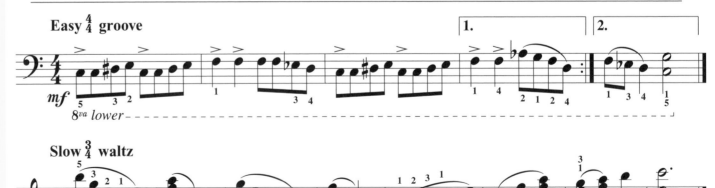

Easy 4/4 groove

mf

8va lower

Slow 3/4 waltz

p

1-2-3, the Pearl is in the C!

Circle all the **Bass C's** in the border.

Hint: Remember to count down 3 spaces.

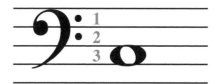

Ex.

■ Draw **4 quarter notes** on Bass C.

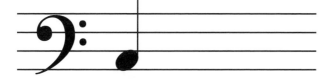

Circle your best!

■ Draw **4 half notes** on Bass C.

Circle your best!

■ Draw **4 dotted half notes** on Bass C.

Circle your best!

■ Draw **4 whole notes** on Bass C.

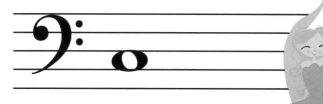

Circle your best!

 Where's Tap?

The Little Scale that Could

C 5-Finger Scale for Bass Staff

Practice this L.H. melody at *slow, medium,* and *fast* speeds.
Play on firm fingertips, and keep the beat steady!

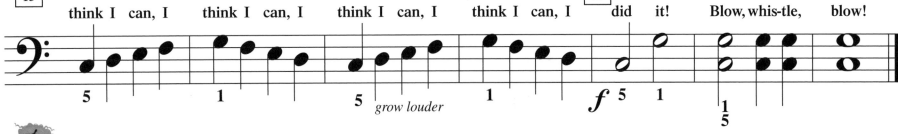

Teacher Duet: (Student plays *as written*.)

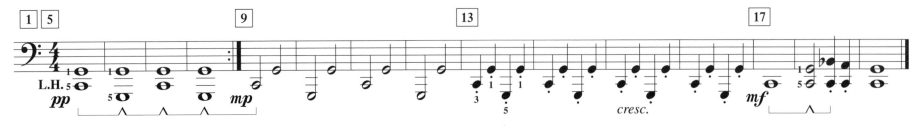

CLAP for Sightreading

LOOK

Eye-training:

1. Lightly color the measure red that matches the **alphabet letters on the left**.

2. Next, sightread each row of measures going across for a **bass C melody**.

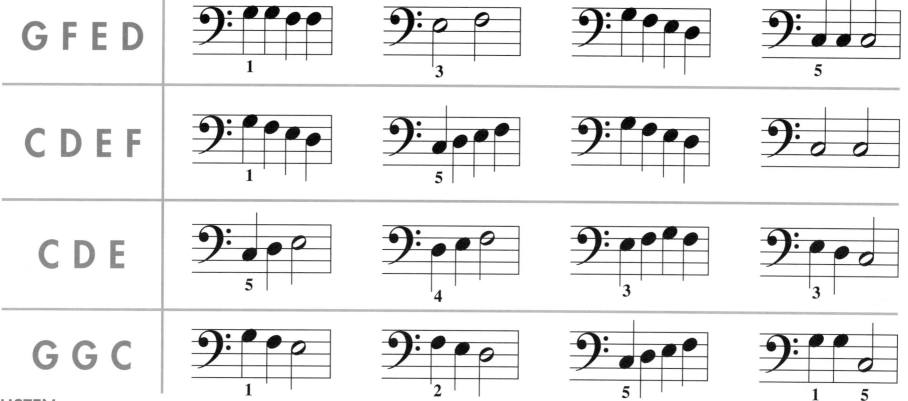

G F E D   1   3   5

C D E F   1   5

C D E   5   4   3   3

G G C   1   2   5   1   5

LISTEN

Ear-training:

Your teacher will play a measure from each line.
Color that measure green (or other color of your choice).

The String Quartet

Rhythm, Reading, and Ensemble Activity

1. Add **bar lines** to each part.

2. Write **letter names** above the notes for *Violin 2* and *Viola*.

Ludwig van Beethoven
Theme from the 9th Symphony

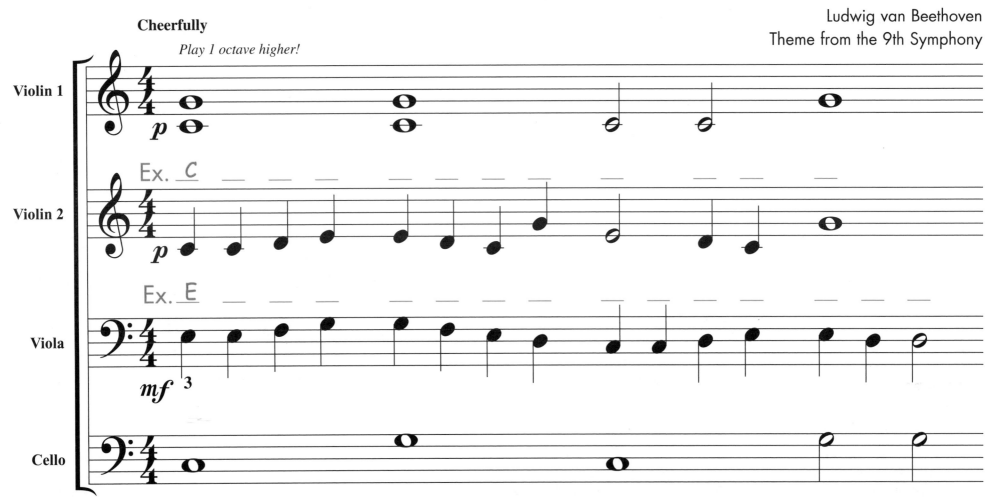

Did you know…

A string quartet has 4 instruments.

2 violins—the highest sounding instruments
that are held under the chin.

1 viola—like a larger, lower sounding violin,
also held under the chin.

1 cello—the lower sounding instrument
that rests on the floor.

Can you answer…

Who is playing the **cello**?

Who are playing the **violins**?

Who is playing the **viola**?

3. Now, sightread each line while your teacher plays one or more of the parts.
Perhaps you can form a quartet with 3 other piano students!

♩ Where's Tap?

Buying Hot Chocolate
Counting the Tie

The Tie

A tie is a curved line connecting 2 notes on the same line or space.

A tie means the note will be played once but held for the length of both notes combined.

3 beats total

Pretend you are buying a cup of hot chocolate. **Each beat = one penny 1¢** .

1. Write the total number of beats for each **tie**.

2. Now connect each cup of hot chocolate to the matching number of pennies below.

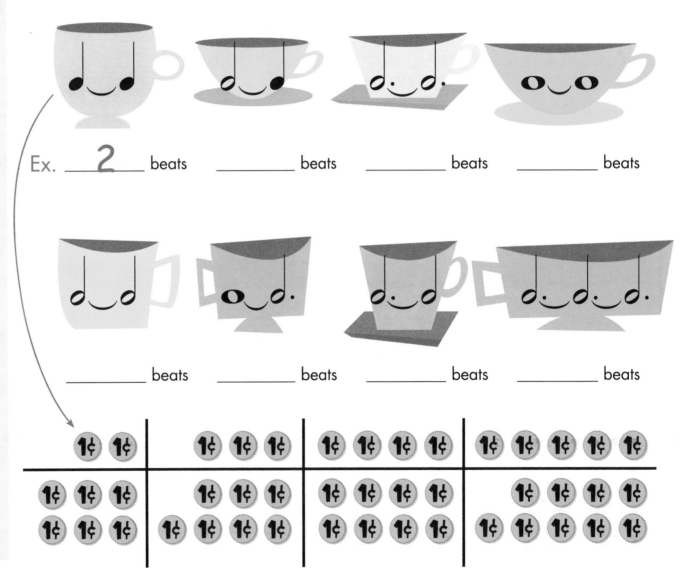

Ex. ___2___ beats   _____ beats   _____ beats   _____ beats

_____ beats   _____ beats   _____ beats   _____ beats

LISTEN

Let's Play Playback!
Hearing Patterns

Ear-training:

1. Place your L.H. in the **C 5-finger scale** on the piano.
   Close your eyes. Your teacher will play a set of notes on a lower C scale.

2. *Feel* the rhythm and play back what you hear.

Draw a "happy face" on a cup of hot chocolate each time you do this activity.

For Teacher Use Only: Play an octave lower. (The examples may be repeated several times.)
The teacher may create more examples on his/her own.

LOOK

CLAP for Sightreading

Eye-training:

1. First, circle the **time signature**.
   Now add bar lines to "cage in the cat."

2. Write the letters to spell C L A P in each box.

COUNT and clap the rhythm.

LOOK at the first notes. Is each on a line or space?
Find your hand placement on the piano.

ATTENTION on what's next!
Up, down, or same?

PLAY. To begin, set a steady beat
by saying "1-2-3 GO."

Pussycat, Pussycat

Traditional words

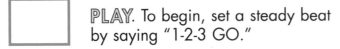

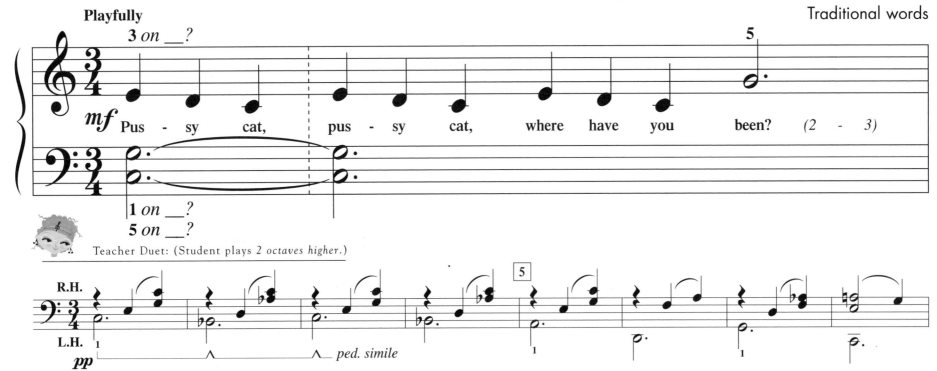

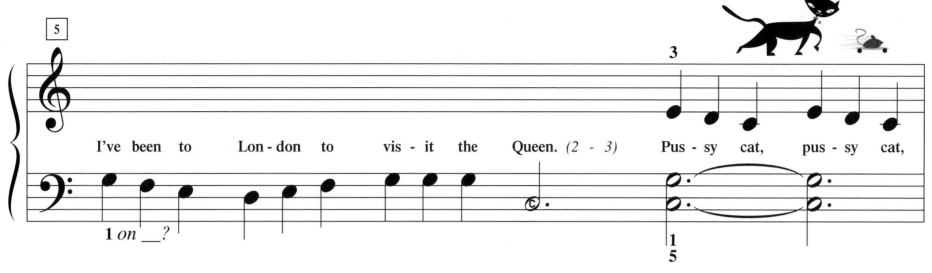

I've been to Lon - don to vis - it the Queen. *(2 - 3)* Pus - sy cat, pus - sy cat,

1 *on __?*

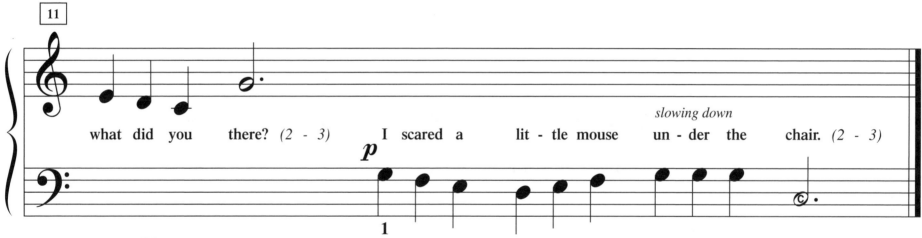

what did you there? *(2 - 3)* I scared a lit - tle mouse un - der the chair. *(2 - 3)*

p

slowing down

Mitsy's Wish

While your teacher plays the duet, would you *improvise* a "royal kitty-cat melody"?
Use any notes of the **C 5-finger scale**. To end, slow down and play a C.

mf   *pp*   *rit.*   *8va*

Wishbone Wish

Rhythm Activity with Quarter Rests

3. Circle a wishbone each time you do this activity.

Quarter Rest

means silence for **1 beat**.

Trace these quarter rests.

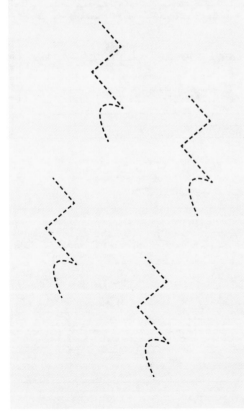

1. Tap the rhythm for *Wishbone Wish* with your teacher.
   Your teacher will chant the words.

2. For the **quarter rest**, quickly make a *loose* fist.

Words by Crystal Bowman

Moderately

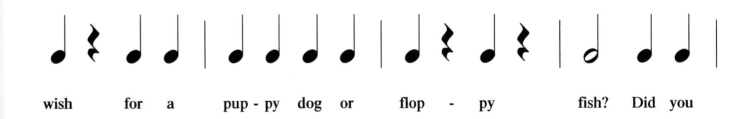

Did *(rest)* you *(rest)* ev - er make a wish - bone wish? Did you

wish for a pup - py dog or flop - py fish? Did you

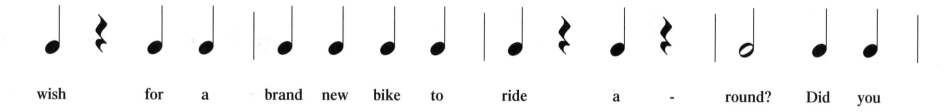

wish   for   a   brand   new   bike   to   ride   a   -   round?   Did   you

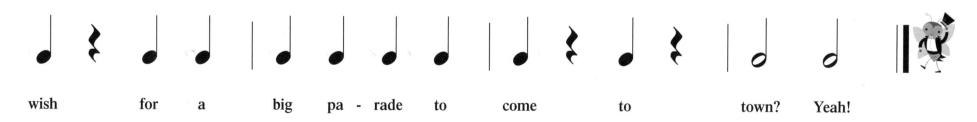

wish   for   a   big   pa - rade   to   come   to   town?   Yeah!

LISTEN

Ear-training:

Your teacher will set the metronome ticking at ♩ = 96.
Together, tap *Wishbone Wish,* listening to the steady tick.
Draw a big "happy face" to show you did it!

Rhythm Beads
Discovering Rhythm Patterns

Your friends have made "rhythm beads." Each string has a **hidden rhythm pattern** that repeats over and over.

LOOK

Eye-training:

1. First, find and circle the **rhythm pattern** for each string.

2. Now write the correct **time signature** in the box *before* each string: $\frac{4}{4}$ or $\frac{3}{4}$

3. Tap each string of rhythm beads. Count aloud!

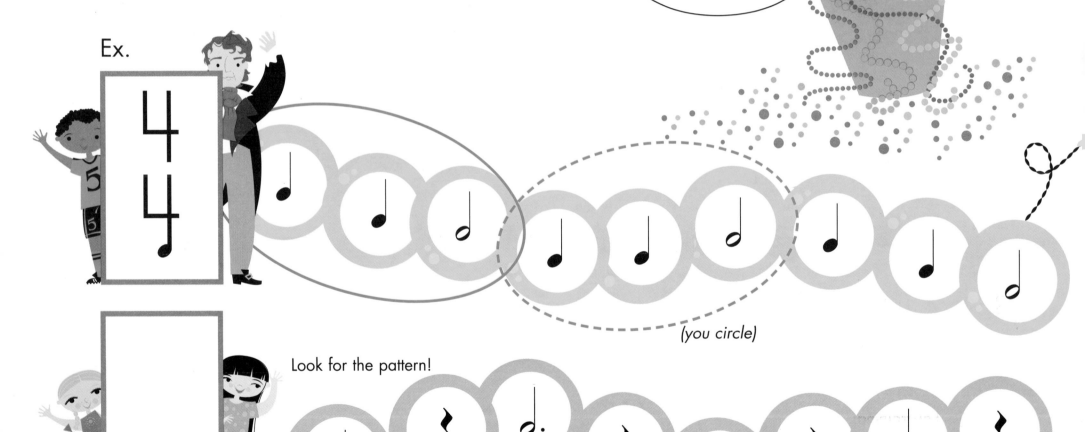

Ex.

(you circle)

Look for the pattern!

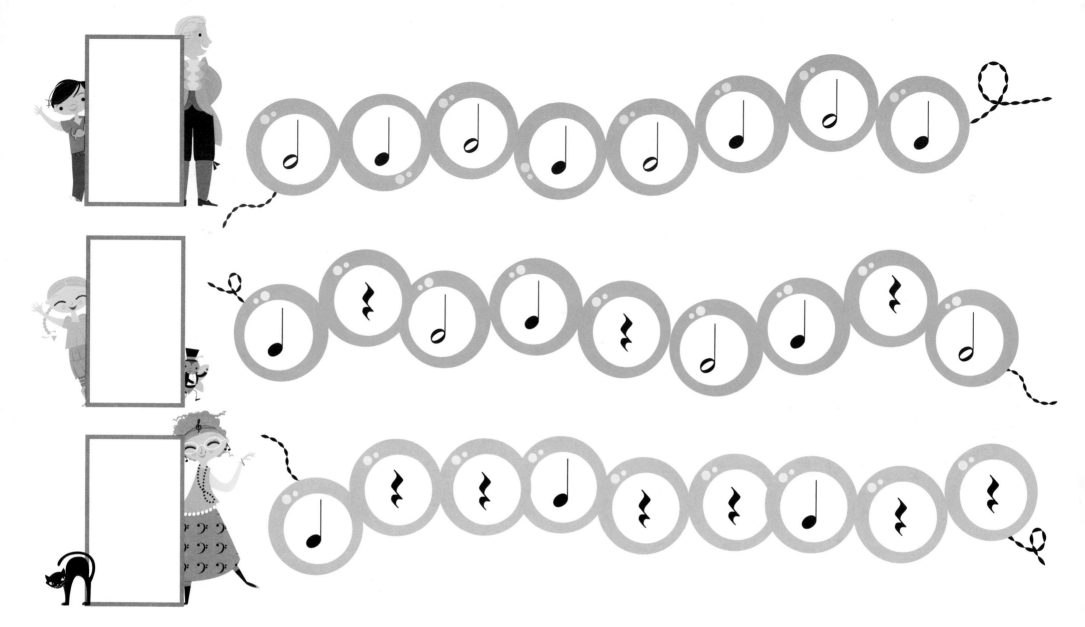

LISTEN

Ear-training:

Your teacher will tap a string of rhythm beads.
Listen and point to the rhythm that you heard.

Teacher Note: You may wish to limit the choice to two rhythms. "Is it the purple beads or the blue beads?"

Travel, Travel Little Car

Twinkle, Twinkle for Left Hand

Tips from your friends:

1. Trace the first bar line. Now add **bar lines** to the rest of the piece.

2. Write the **note names** in the squares.

3. Play as a solo and with the duet. (Your teacher will show you the crossover in *measures 1–2*.)

With a steady beat

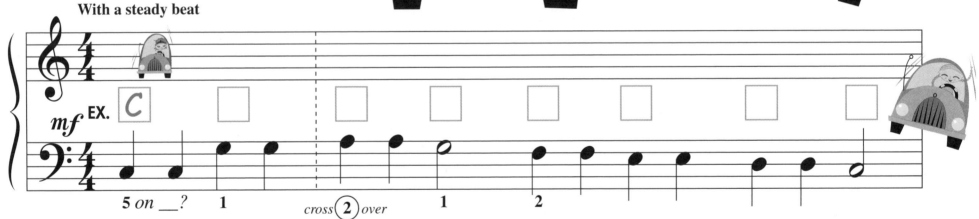

mf **EX.** C

5 *on* __ ?   1   *cross* ② *over*   1   2

Teacher Duet: (Student plays *as written*.)

| 1 | 9 |

Fine

L.H.

mp

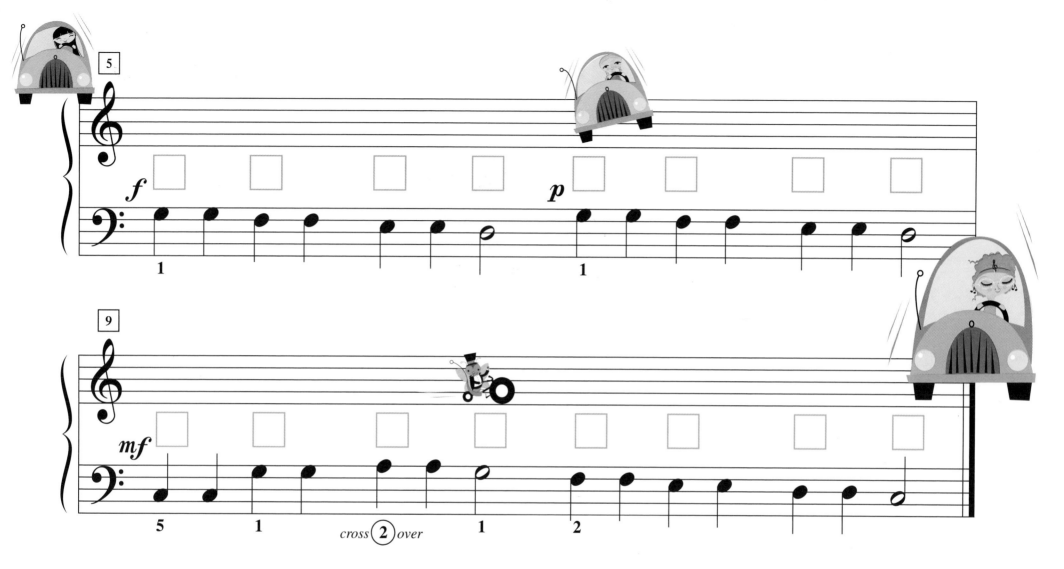

4. Point out the following to your teacher:
   treble clef, bass clef, time signature, *mf*, *f*, and *p* signs,
   repeated notes, step up, step down, and double bar line.

♩ Where's Tap?

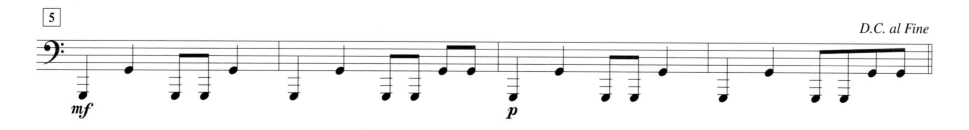

Congratulations

(Sign and join the club!)

Tip from Tap:

Start at the owl,
and connect the numbers
for a surprise!

You have completed
My First Piano Adventure® Writing Book B.

Get your pencil ready for Writing Book C!

FF1622